The Second Continental Congress

by Jessica Gunderson

Content Adviser: Richard J. Bell, Ph.D.,
Assistant Professor, Department of History,
University of Maryland

Reading Adviser: Alexa L. Sandmann, Ph.D.,
Associate Professor of Literacy,
Kent State University

Compass Point Books ✦ Minneapolis, Minnesota

Compass Point Books
3109 West 50th Street, #115
Minneapolis, MN 55410

This book was manufactured with paper containing
at least 10 percent post-consumer waste.

On the cover: The Second Continental Congress appointed George Washington
as commander in chief; 1876 lithograph by Currier & Ives

Editor: Jennifer VanVoorst
Page Production: Ashlee Schultz
Photo Researcher: Svetlana Zhurkin
Cartographer: XNR Productions, Inc.
Library Consultant: Kathleen Baxter

Creative Director: Keith Griffin
Editorial Director: Nick Healy
Managing Editor: Catherine Neitge

Library of Congress Cataloging-in-Publication Data
Gunderson, Jessica.
  The Second Continental Congress / by Jessica Gunderson.
    p. cm. — (We the people)
  Includes bibliographical references and index.
  ISBN 978-0-7565-3639-8 (library binding)
  1. United States. Continental Congress—History—Juvenile literature. 2. United States—Politics and
government—1775–1783—Juvenile literature. 3. United States—History—Revolution, 1775–1783—
Juvenile literature. I. Title. II. Series.
  E303.G86 2008
  973.3'12—dc22   2007035564

Visit Compass Point Books on the Internet at *www.compasspointbooks.com*
or e-mail your request to *custserv@compasspointbooks.com*

TABLE OF CONTENTS

"No Taxation Without Representation!"

May 10, 1775, seemed like an ordinary day in Philadelphia, Pennsylvania. Sunlight weaved through the trees. Birds chirped. To the 51 men gathered at the State House, however, the day was anything but ordinary. An important task lay ahead of them. These men were about to determine the future of the American colonies.

Eight months earlier, many of the same men had met in what was known as the First Continental Congress. Their goal was to repair the relationship between the American colonies and England, the mother country. American colonists were angry with England's King George III because of the taxes he had been forcing the colonies to pay. To make matters worse, America was not allowed to participate in Parliament, England's governing body. All across the colonies, cries of "No taxation without representation!" could be heard.

Colonists gathered to discuss and protest British treatment.

The king had his reasons for taxing the colonies. From 1754 to 1763, England and France had fought for control of North America in the French and Indian War. Though France's surrender gave the English a victory, the war hurt the English economy. The king raised taxes on the American colonies to help pay war debts. The king and Parliament decided the taxes were fair. After all, the war had been fought over the land the colonists lived on.

King George III

American colonists, however, felt they were being ruled by an unfair leader who ignored their rights. They had no say over the rules that were imposed on them. Some colonists refused to pay the taxes. Some also boycotted English products. Instead of lowering taxes, England passed even stricter laws on the Americans. The Townshend Act, for example, taxed glass, paper, paint, and tea.

Something had to be done. The colonists were unhappy about what they considered to be unfair treatment. Some colonists, such as Samuel Adams and Patrick Henry,

Patrick Henry protested British taxation practices to Virginia lawmakers.

spoke up angrily. They formed groups, such as the Sons of Liberty and Daughters of Liberty, that protested taxation.

Leaders in the various colonies realized that they needed to communicate with each other and unite in their efforts in order to be heard by England. They wrote letters to each other, which were carried from one town to another by fast riders like Paul Revere.

In the event known as the Boston Tea Party, colonists dumped tea overboard to protest English taxation.

The colonial leaders soon realized that letters weren't enough. They needed to meet in person to discuss what to do about England. In the meantime, England passed more laws, such as the Coercive Acts in 1774 that punished the people of Massachusetts.

Frustrated with the king's treatment, leaders organized a congress, or meeting. The meeting later became known as the First Continental Congress.

COLONIES IN REBELLION

Each of the 13 colonies except Georgia sent delegates to the First Continental Congress, which was held in Philadelphia. The men met in secret. If the English government found out about the meeting, the delegates could have been accused of treason.

Most delegates wanted to repair the ties with England. Declaring independence from the mother country

Delegates to the First Continental Congress opened their meeting with a prayer on September 5, 1774.

9

was not seriously considered. They wrote a letter to King George explaining how they felt about the laws he and Parliament had passed. Many of the delegates were sure the king would listen to them and repeal the punishing laws.

They were wrong. The king didn't even read the letter. He refused to recognize the Congress as a valid organization. Basically, he ignored the issue. It was the worst thing he could have done.

The First Continental Congress met at Philadelphia's Carpenters' Hall.

The First Continental Congress decided that America should halt all trade with England. The Congress adjourned in October 1774 and agreed to meet again the following May to discuss the king's response.

Before that meeting, though, another problem arose. On April 19, 1775, British troops marched toward Concord, Massachusetts, to seize ammunition the Americans had stored there. Local militia, known as Minutemen, gathered their rifles. They met the British soldiers at Lexington. A shot was fired, and the battle began. This battle and

The Battle of Lexington was the opening battle of the Revolutionary War.

the one that followed later that day, known as the Battles of Lexington and Concord, were the first battles of what would become the Revolutionary War.

The Second Continental Congress convened on May 10, 1775. The delegates at Philadelphia's State House shifted uncomfortably in their seats. The room was hot. Their palms sweated. They had so many decisions to make that they did not know where to begin. And now, men's lives were at stake. Rebellion had taken hold of the colonies, and war was on its way.

The Second Continental Congress met at Philadelphia's State House, now known as Independence Hall.

THE CONTINENTAL ARMY

At first, no one at the Second Continental Congress mentioned independence. So many other questions filled their minds. Should they make one last attempt to make peace with England? Should they organize a military? What was the next step?

Each delegate had different ideas to contribute to the discussion. They had come from various backgrounds and occupations. Some were lawyers. Others were landowners, planters, and merchants. Almost all of them had wealth and power. Some of the most influential delegates were John Adams, Samuel Adams, John Hancock, and John Dickinson. Other powerful delegates were Benjamin Franklin, Richard Henry Lee, and Thomas Jefferson.

Even though they knew the colonies needed leadership, many delegates were hesitant to take control. After all, they had not come together to form a ruling body. They didn't want to make decisions for the colonies that

13

John Adams (from left), Gouverneur Morris, and Thomas Jefferson (standing) were among the leaders of the Second Continental Congress. Alexander Hamilton (second from right) was an influential member of later Congresses.

the colonists hadn't voted on. So they decided to read all the letters and newspapers they received from each of the 13 colonies. This took a lot of time and the meetings moved slowly, but every voice was heard.

As battles raged in Massachusetts and other colonies, Congress decided to organize an army. Many of the colonies had their own militias. But Congress knew that a united Continental Army would help America stand its ground against the British. First, though, the Continental Army needed a top commander.

Thomas Johnson of Maryland nominated George Washington, a delegate from Virginia. Washington had shown military skill when he fought in the French and Indian War. John Adams of Massachusetts seconded the motion. The rest of the delegates voted, and each voted in favor of George Washington.

Every army needs supplies and wages for its soldiers, but the colonies didn't have much money. How would they fund the patriot cause?

George Washington was unanimously elected to lead the Continental Army.

15

Printing paper money was one idea. They didn't have gold to back up the money, but what else were they to do? Congress approved the idea, and paper bills called Continentals were printed. Because there was no gold to back up the bills, though, the decision would cause problems later in the war.

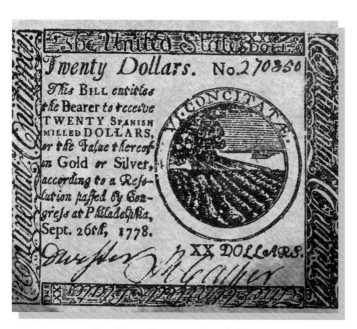

Continentals were printed for currency during the Revolutionary War.

Even though America was in conflict against England, some delegates wanted to make one last effort to restore harmony. Battles such as Lexington and Concord and Bunker Hill had shown that the colonists were willing to fight for their rights. Surely King George would listen this time.

So in July 1775, John Dickinson of Pennsylvania wrote the Olive Branch Petition. In this document, he made suggestions on how to resolve the conflicts between the colonies and England. However, the king rejected the deal for peace. Instead, he declared that the colonies were in a state of rebellion and ordered his soldiers to stop the revolt.

John Dickinson hoped the Olive Branch Petition would end the conflict between the colonies and England.

The king's response caused a single thought to take hold in the minds of the delegates: independence.

17

VOICES OF INDEPENDENCE

Before they could announce independence from England, the Continental Congress had to think of the peoples' wishes. Not everyone wanted independence. Some colonists still believed the colonies should remain under English rule.

Thomas Paine's booklet, Common Sense, *promoted the cause of independence.*

Southern colonies, especially, worried that independence would hurt the economy.

A man named Thomas Paine changed many colonists' minds. In January 1776, he published a booklet called *Common Sense.* He called King George a "royal brute" and wrote that America should separate from England. The pamphlet became extremely popular and helped spread the idea of freedom throughout the colonies.

Virginia delegate Richard Henry Lee wrote a resolution that outlined America's desire for independence. Many delegates supported the resolution, but John Dickinson spoke out against independence. He said that Americans had enjoyed liberty under the king. He was concerned that breaking away from England would cause more trouble.

Richard Henry Lee

The only course of action was to take a vote on the resolution for independence. First, though, Congress appointed Virginia delegate Thomas Jefferson to write a formal statement declaring independence. When he was finished, they could vote on Lee's

Thomas Jefferson

19

resolution and Jefferson's document.

Jefferson was a quiet man of 33 who hadn't had as much political experience as some of the other delegates. He asked John Adams why he had been chosen to write such an important document.

Benjamin Franklin and John Adams helped Thomas Jefferson (right) revise the Declaration of Independence.

"You can write ten times better than I can," Adams replied.

"Well," said Jefferson, "if you are decided, I will do as well as I can."

Jefferson was true to his word. He spent several days in a tiny rented room writing the Declaration of Independence. He rewrote it many times, taking suggestions from other members of the Congress.

In late June, Jefferson brought the final draft of the Declaration of Independence to the Congress. It was time to vote on whether to declare independence.

Some colonies, such as South Carolina and Pennsylvania, wanted to stay under England's rule. However, their local governments told the

A draft of the Declaration of Independence shows changes Jefferson made to the document.

delegates to agree to what Congress thought was best for America. Other colonies, like New York, were waiting for direction from colony leaders.

Colonial leaders approved the Declaration of Independence on July 4, 1776.

On July 2, delegates from every colony except New York voted in favor of independence. New York delegates had not heard from colony leaders and so did not vote.

Two days later, on July 4, 1776, the Second Continental Congress approved the formal document, the Declaration of Independence. The 13 colonies became the United States of America.

When word spread that independence had been officially declared, people rejoiced. The colonies were still at war, but now the war was being fought for a higher cause: life, liberty, and the pursuit of happiness.

THE ARTICLES OF CONFEDERATION

The young country needed a new government. A year before independence, Pennsylvania delegate Benjamin Franklin had proposed a plan for governing the colonies. At that time, most of Congress thought Franklin's plan was not needed.

Now, though, a plan was needed, and quickly. Congress organized a committee to draft a plan for the government. The committee was headed by John Dickinson. Even though Dickinson had been opposed to independence, he was loyal

Benjamin Franklin

23

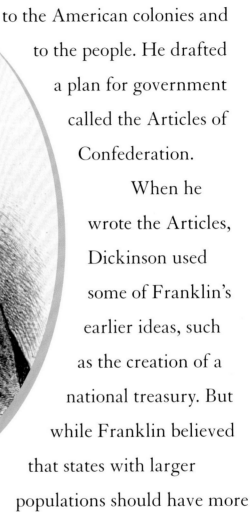

John Dickinson

to the American colonies and to the people. He drafted a plan for government called the Articles of Confederation.

When he wrote the Articles, Dickinson used some of Franklin's earlier ideas, such as the creation of a national treasury. But while Franklin believed that states with larger populations should have more representatives in Congress, Dickinson felt that each state should have one representative, regardless of its population.

Dickinson presented Congress with his finished draft of the Articles on July 12, 1776. The delegates argued over

24

Under the Articles of Confederation, each state received one vote in Congress.

a number of the ideas presented in the document. Many of the states wanted their own rights. They did not want to be controlled by a strong national government, like they had been by England. Others insisted that a strong government

25

was necessary. They believed that if each state had too much power, the country could become divided.

A balance of power was important to everyone. The challenge was finding a way to balance the powers of the states and the nation.

The delegates wrote and rewrote sections of the Articles of Confederation until they found a compromise. The new federal government would be extremely limited. Individual states would have power to create their own laws and taxes. Like Dickinson wanted, each

The first page of the Articles of Confederation

state would have one representative in Congress. There would be no national president.

Because each state created its own taxes, the federal government could not require the states to pay taxes. Also, the new government could not force the states to send troops to fight the war.

Many delegates saw problems with the Articles of Confederation. For example, one vote for each state was good for smaller states. But larger states had a problem with it because they felt their population wasn't

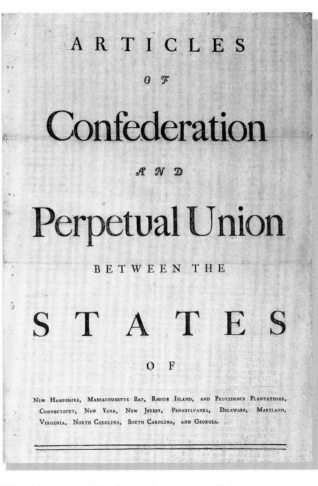

The title page of the first printed copy of the Articles of Confederation

27

being represented fairly.

Even though the Articles of Confederation had problems, most delegates agreed that the plan would work—at least for the time being. They could always change it if they encountered difficulties.

The Articles had to be approved by each state's government, not just the delegates. This would take a long time, so the Second Continental Congress began governing the nation under the Articles even before it was ratified. It took five years for every state to ratify the document.

TROUBLES IN CONGRESS

In December 1776, General Washington sent a warning to the Congress. The British army was advancing quickly toward Philadelphia. If members of Congress were captured or killed by the British, their plans for America could be ruined.

A move to a new meeting place seemed necessary, even though some delegates thought that such a move would make Congress seem cowardly to the American people and the British. In the end, though, Congress decided it was best to retreat to Baltimore, Maryland.

General George Washington

As the war progressed, Congress relocated four more times: When Philadelphia was safe again, Congress moved back to the State House. But in September 1777, the meeting was moved to Lancaster, Pennsylvania, and then York, Pennsylvania. Finally, in 1778, Congress returned to Philadelphia.

The Second Continental Congress met inside Philadelphia's State House, now Independence Hall.

A major problem Congress faced during these years was the cost of the war. Early in the war, the delegates had approved issuing $2 million to fund the war for that year. Within only a few months, however, the money was used up. Congress had to approve more funding.

Continentals were still being printed as money. They had lost value, though, mostly because of counterfeiting and the lack of gold to back up the bills.

Because of the shortage of money, Congress had a difficult time providing supplies for the troops. Soldiers had only small amounts of food. Most of the time, they ate a fried mixture of flour and water. They craved meat and vegetables. The soldiers also desperately needed clothing and boots. Some had to wear rags on their feet because they had no shoes. As if these conditions weren't bad enough, many of the soldiers were not being paid.

The British army knew that the Continental Army was low on supplies. They attacked and destroyed storerooms full of salted meat, flour, and gunpowder.

31

Soldiers in the Continental Army suffered through the cold winter of 1777–1778 with little food or clothing while camped at Valley Forge.

Congress was troubled by the unhappiness of the soldiers. Financial support was desperately needed. The congressional delegates knew they had to turn to other countries and ask for help.

A CALL TO NATIONS

Early in the war, Congress had sent a message to neighboring Canada asking for support. Canada was part of the British Empire. If Canada joined the revolution, America would have a much better chance of winning the war.

But Canada decided to remain loyal to England. During the war, Canada harbored many British soldiers. Also, many Americans who were still loyal to England, called loyalists or Tories, had fled to Canada.

Those loyalists who favored England in the Revolutionary War were often ridiculed by other colonists.

33

Congress also approached American Indian tribes, asking that they remain neutral. "Brothers and friends," the delegates told tribal leaders, "this is a family quarrel between us and Old England. You are not concerned in it." Even so, many Indian tribes joined British troops.

European support was the most crucial. Congress formed the Committee of Secret Correspondence, later

Mohawk Indians joined British troops to fight American colonists at Oriskany, New York.

34

known as the Committee for Foreign Affairs. Members of the committee traveled to France, Spain, Russia, and other countries to gain support for America's cause.

France, a longtime enemy of England, rushed to America's aid. The French sent 6,000 soldiers to help the Americans fight the war. France also loaned money to the United States to help with war expenses. Without the

Congressional delegates greeted the first French minister to America after signing the Treaty of Alliance in 1778.

support of France, independence might never have
been won.

On October 24, 1781, a breathless rider arrived at the
State House carrying a letter from General Washington.
Several days earlier, the letter explained, British General
Charles Cornwallis had surrendered at Yorktown. The war

*The British surrendered to General George Washington
following the Battle of Yorktown in Virginia.*

was nearing its end.

Though the majority of the fighting was indeed over, the conflict was not. Peace agreements needed to be made. Representatives from both England and America met in Paris, France. There, in 1783, they signed the Treaty of Paris. The treaty stated that England would recognize the United States as an independent country. In return, English merchants would be repaid their debts, and England would keep control of Canada.

The Treaty of Paris was signed by British representative David Hartley and Americans John Adams, Benjamin Franklin, and John Jay.

THE NEW CONGRESS

In 1781, after the Articles of Confederation were ratified, the Second Continental Congress became "The United States in Congress Assembled." The Second Continental Congress formally adjourned on March 1, 1781.

The new Congress had quite a few problems to deal with after the war. Most of its time was spent settling arguments between the states, a tedious task. Not much else got done, and many delegates were frustrated.

Foreign countries were also frustrated with the United States. Each state had its own trade regulations. These regulations differed from state to state. The different rules were confusing to countries that traded with the United States.

Finally, in 1787, some delegates met to discuss what they should do. Government under the Articles of Confederation just wasn't working. They agreed that a new plan of government should be written.

Later that year, the Constitutional Convention was held. Its delegates drafted the United States Constitution, the document that states the basic laws and principles by which the United States is governed.

With the Constitution, the new country would now have a stronger central government. Congress would also now have two governing bodies, the House of Representatives and the Senate. Like Benjamin Franklin

The U.S. Constitution was signed on September 17, 1787.

The Constitution is the primary governing document of the United States of America.

had originally wanted, each state would be represented in the House according to population. And, like John Dickinson had wanted, each state would elect two representatives to serve in the Senate.

The Constitution also stated that there would be a chief executive officer, or president, to lead the country. Congress met one last time in October 1788 to decide who should be the first president of the United States. That man, Congress concluded, was General George Washington.

The Second Continental Congress made many achievements during the six years it met. It declared

George Washington was inaugurated as president on April 30, 1789.

independence and agreed upon a representative form of government rather than a monarchy. The decisions made by the members of this Congress helped form the United States the world knows today.

Even though the Second Continental Congress adjourned in 1781, the work of the delegates was not over. Many of them went on to serve as representatives, senators, or judges. Some became governors. Some even became president. And all became known throughout history as America's Founding Fathers.

GLOSSARY

adjourned—suspended indefinitely or until a later time

boycotted—refused to do business with someone as a form of protest

colonies—the 13 British territories that became the United States of America

compromise—agreement that is reached after people with opposing views give up some of their demands

Constitution—the document that describes the basic laws and principles by which the United States is governed

counterfeiting—making an illegal copy of something

delegate—person who represents other people at a meeting

militia—military force, often made up of volunteers

patriot—an American colonist who favored independence from Britain; patriots are people who love their country

ratified—formally approved

DID YOU KNOW?

- No women served in the Continental Congress. Women weren't even allowed to vote in the United States until 1920.

- In his original draft of the Declaration of Independence, Thomas Jefferson condemned slavery. This section was taken out because many delegates who were dependent on slave labor were offended. Even though Jefferson himself owned slaves, he was against the idea of slave trade.

- Spain and the Netherlands, along with France, joined the American Revolution on the side of the United States. Spain, however, refused to recognize the independence of the United States. Spain was afraid that Spanish colonies would start their own revolution for independence.

- Charles Thomson served as secretary during the Continental Congress and kept a journal of each day's proceedings. By the time Congress adjourned, Thomson had 170,000 written pages.

- John Adams and Thomas Jefferson died on the same day. That day was July 4, 1826, the 50th anniversary of the approval of the Declaration of Independence.

IMPORTANT DATES

Timeline

1763	The French and Indian War ends; England begins imposing taxes on the American colonies.
1772	The Committee of Correspondence communicates by writing letters.
1774	The First Continental Congress meets.
1775	War with England begins with the Battles of Lexington and Concord; the Second Continental Congress meets.
1776	The Declaration of Independence is approved.
1777	The Second Continental Congress adopts the Articles of Confederation.
1781	The states formally ratify the Articles of Confederation; the Second Continental Congress adjourns; the British surrender to General George Washington.
1783	The Treaty of Paris is signed, officially ending the war.
1787	A new Constitution to govern the states is drafted.

IMPORTANT PEOPLE

JOHN ADAMS (1735–1826)

Patriot leader and second president of the United States; while in Philadelphia for the Congress, Adams wrote long letters to his wife, Abigail, telling of the day's events

JOHN DICKINSON (1732–1808)

Author of the Olive Branch Petition and the Articles of Confederation; Dickinson is known as the "Penman of the Revolution"

BENJAMIN FRANKLIN (1706–1790)

Delegate to the Constitutional Convention and ambassador to France; Franklin was also a scientist, writer, and civic leader

THOMAS JEFFERSON (1743–1826)

Author of the Declaration of Independence and third president of the United States; Jefferson was also a scientist, inventor, and architect

GEORGE WASHINGTON (1732–1799)

Virginia planter who was named Commander of the Continental Army during the Revolutionary War and was later elected first president of the United States

WANT TO KNOW MORE?

More Books to Read

Anderson, Dale. *The American Colonies Declare Independence.* Milwaukee:
World Almanac Library, 2006.

Freedman, Russell. *Give Me Liberty!: The Story of the Declaration of
Independence.* New York: Holiday House, 2000.

McNeese, Tim. *George Washington: America's Leader in War and Peace.*
Philadelphia: Chelsea House Publishers, 2006.

On the Web

For more information on this topic, use FactHound.

1. Go to *www.facthound.com*

2. Type in this book ID: 0756536391

3. Click on the *Fetch It* button.

FactHound will find the best Web sites for you.

On the Road

Independence Hall

598 Chestnut St.
Philadelphia, PA 19106
215/597-8974
Building where the Second
Continental Congress met and
the Declaration of Independence
was signed

Liberty Bell

Market Street between Fifth and
Sixth streets
Philadelphia, PA 19106
215/597-8974
Bell that rang throughout
the Revolutionary War and
during the meeting of the Second
Continental Congress

Look for more We the People books about this era:

The Articles of Confederation

The Battle of Bunker Hill

The Battle of Saratoga

The Battles of Lexington and Concord

The Bill of Rights

The Boston Massacre

The Boston Tea Party

The Declaration of Independence

The Electoral College

*Great Women of the American
    Revolution*

Inventions of the 1700s

The Minutemen

Monticello

Mount Vernon

Paul Revere's Ride

The Surrender of Cornwallis

The U.S. Constitution

Valley Forge

A complete list of We the People titles is available on our Web site:
www.compasspointbooks.com

INDEX

About the Author

Jessica Gunderson has written several children's books, both fiction and nonfiction. She especially enjoys historical subjects. Recently she received the Rowland Fellowship from Vermont Studio Center. She lives in a historic house in Madison, Wisconsin, with her husband and cat.